Draw-ma a Llama
An interactive drawing guide for llama lovers

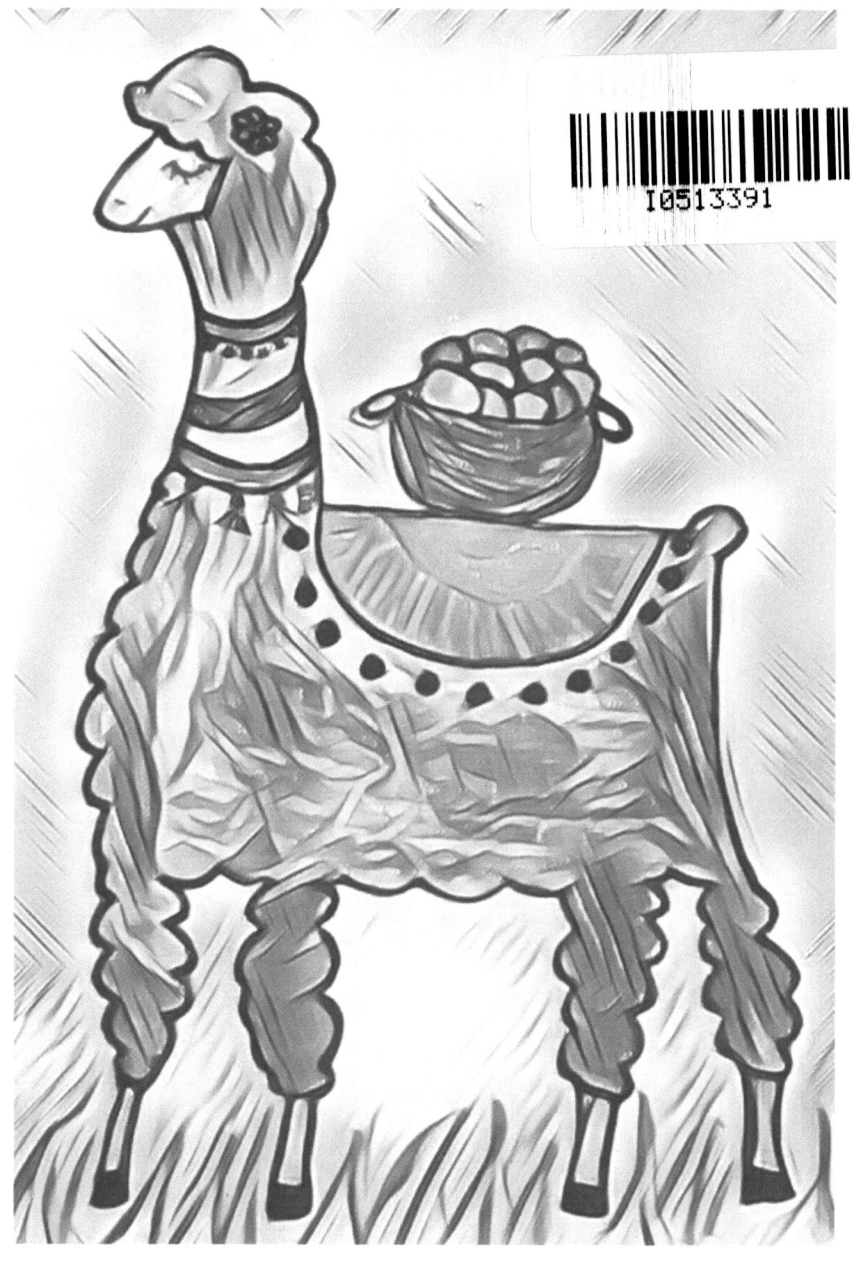

COPYRIGHT © JENNIFER RODRIGUEZ 2019. ALL RIGHTS RESERVED. NO PART OF THIS BOOK MAY BE REPRODUCED OR MODIFIED IN ANY FORM INCLUDING PHOTOCOPYING, RECORDING, OR BY ANY INFORMATION STORAGE AND RETRIEVAL SYSTEM, WITHOUT PERMISSION IN WRITING FROM THE PUBLISHER.

This book is dedicated to my niece, Olivia.

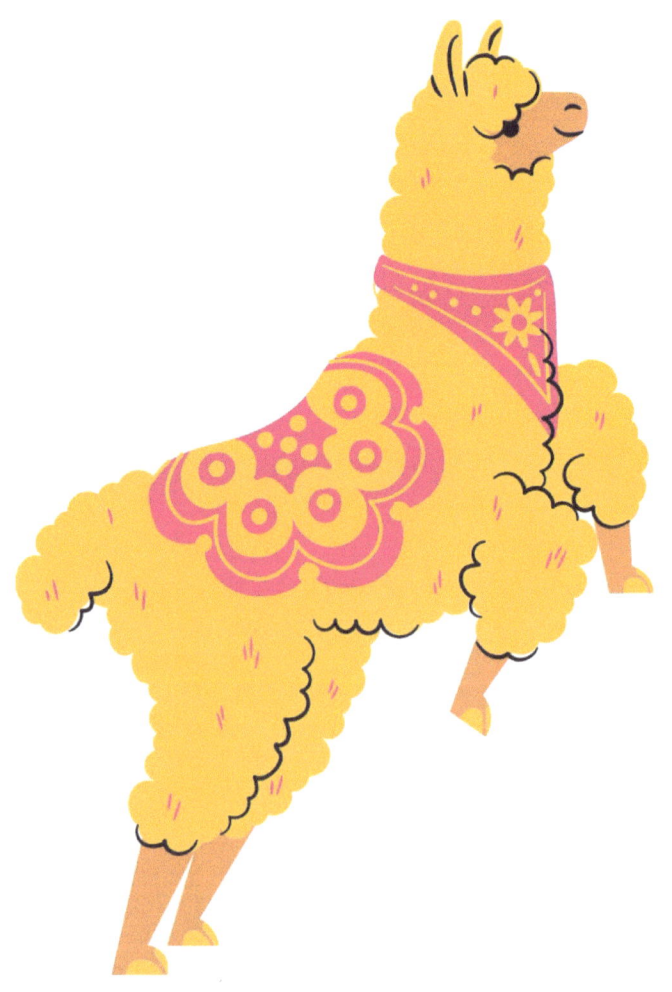

Thanks for being my drawing buddy!

Dear Draw-some Artist,

Thanks for purchasing this book! Maybe you've always wanted to draw a llama, or maybe you've never thought about it before today. That's okay! This book will show you how I like to draw a llama, but I hope you'll share your work with me along the way too! Happy drawing!

Jennifer

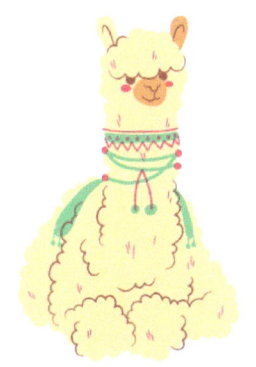

I like to draw a llama in small steps. It helps me to slow down and focus. I also always start with a pencil. I go back over my final lines later with a dark marker or pen, before coloring my llama in!

What you'll need to get started:

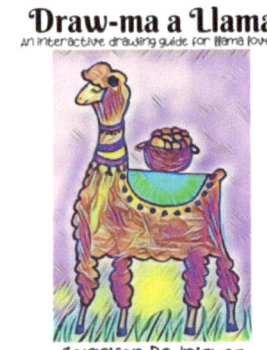 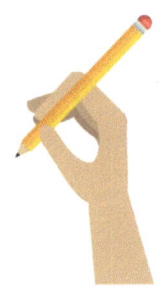 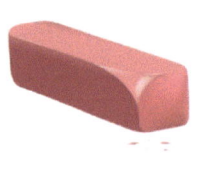

This book!   A sharpened pencil   An eraser

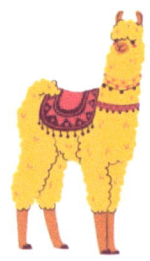

TIP: If your drawing looks different than mine, that's OKAY! We're all different and we do things our own special way!

The first things I like to draw are the back and tail. I think of it as a backwards "L" facing the ground with a small ball in the corner.

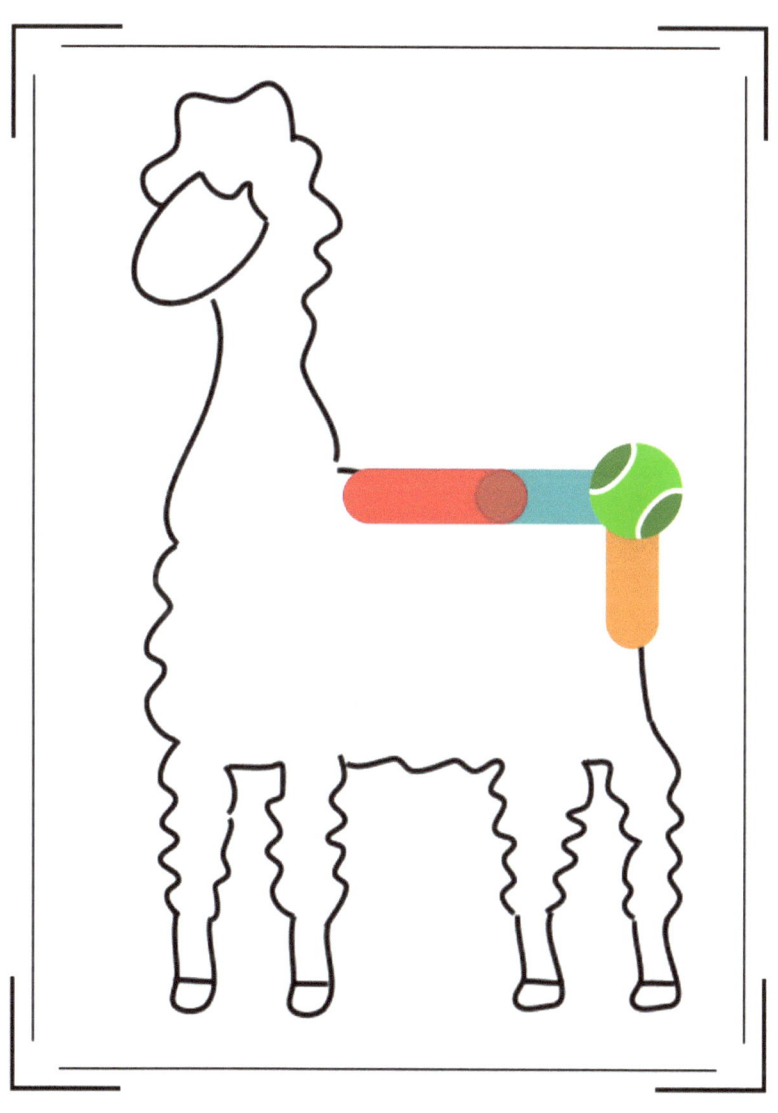

Back & Tail

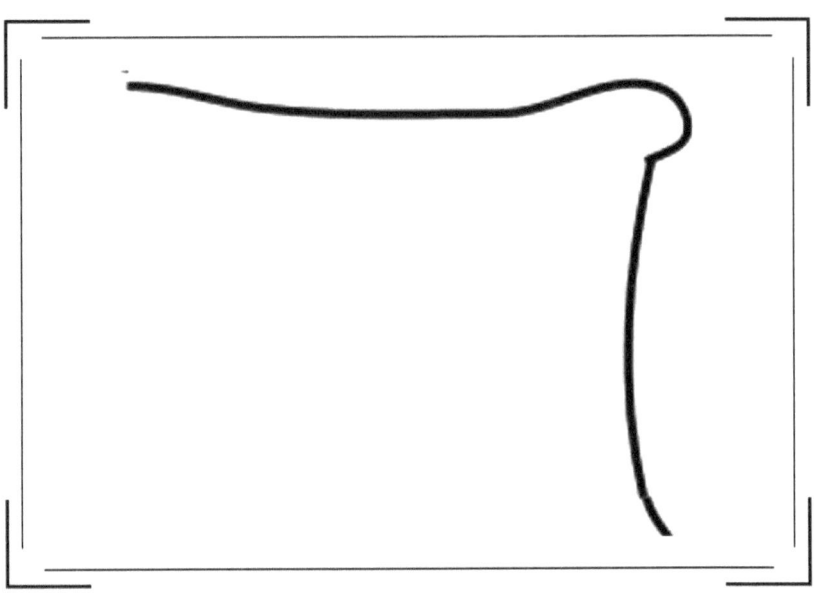

Trace it here!

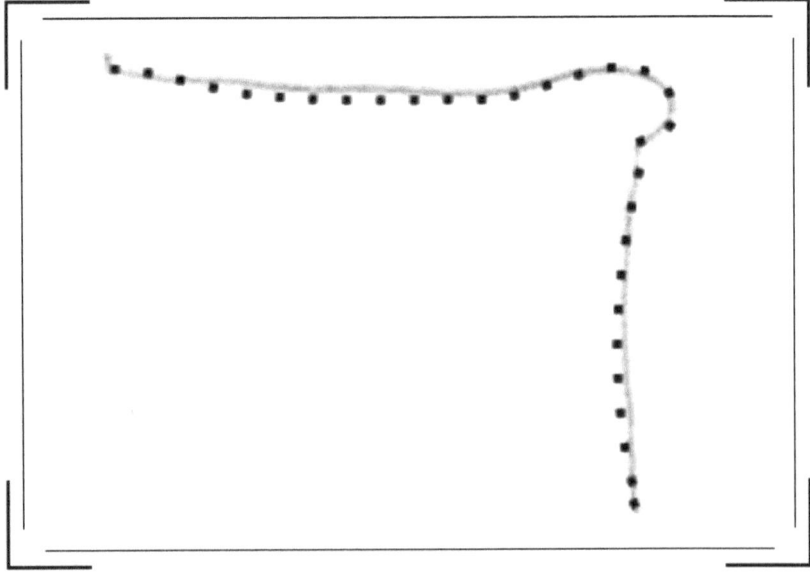

Now you try! What do your back and tail look like? Draw them below.

Next, I like to draw are the neck and head. I think of it as two ice cream cones intersecting. I recommend you draw this part kind of lightly because we will be adding details to the face later!

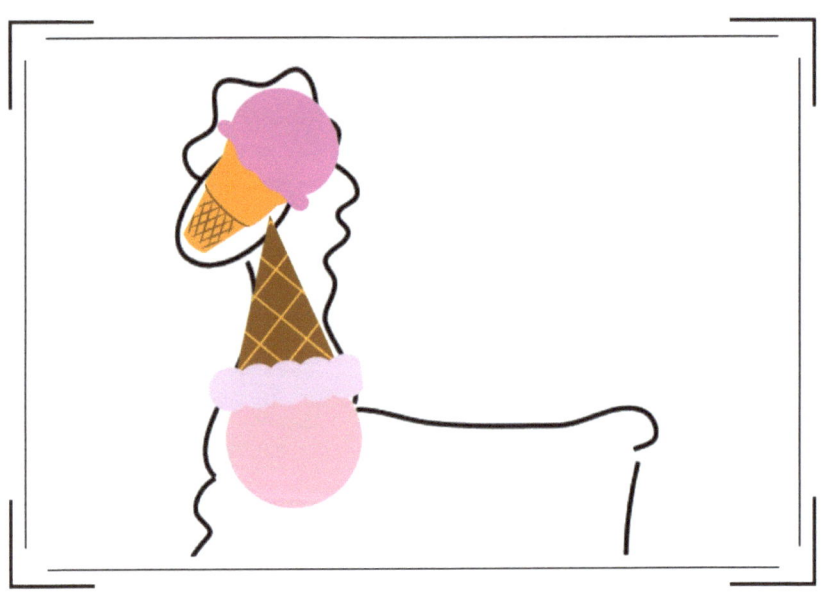

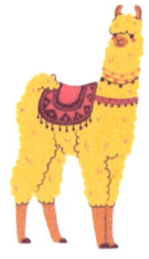

TIP: The angle of the head and neck is up to you! Is the llama standing straight up? Is she leaning down to eat some grass? You are the master of your creation!

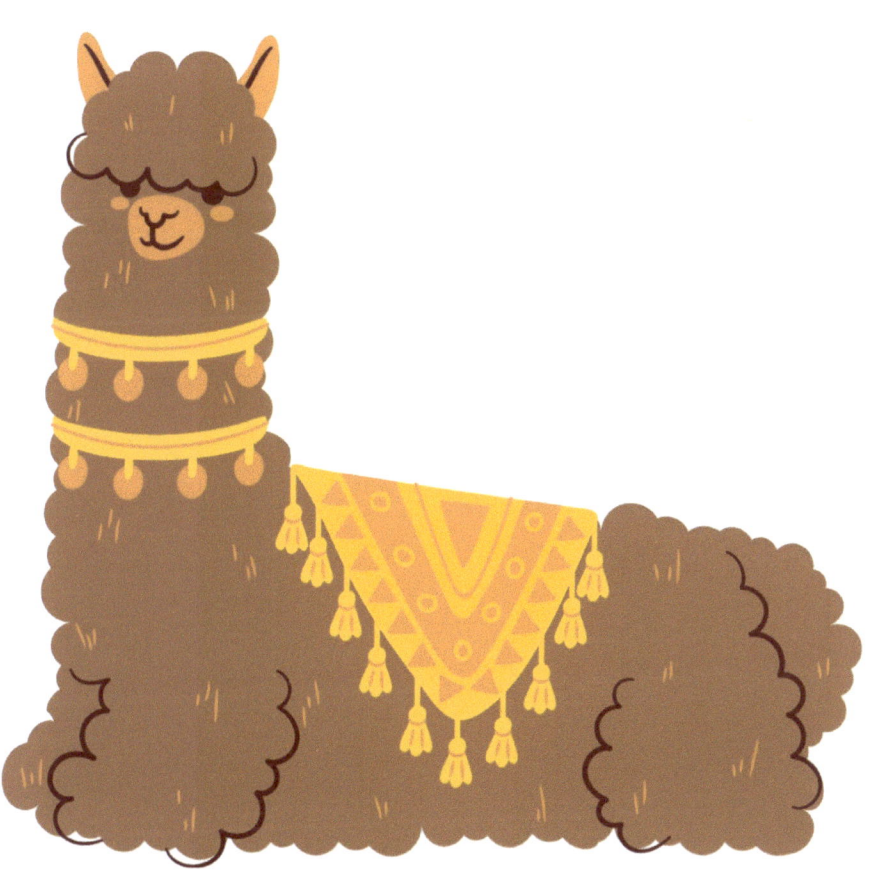

Neck & Head

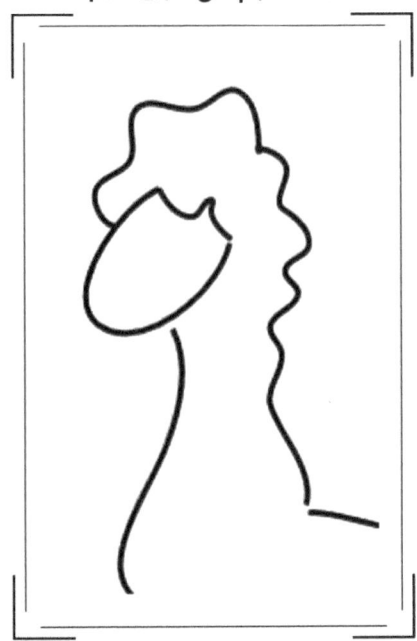

Trace it here!

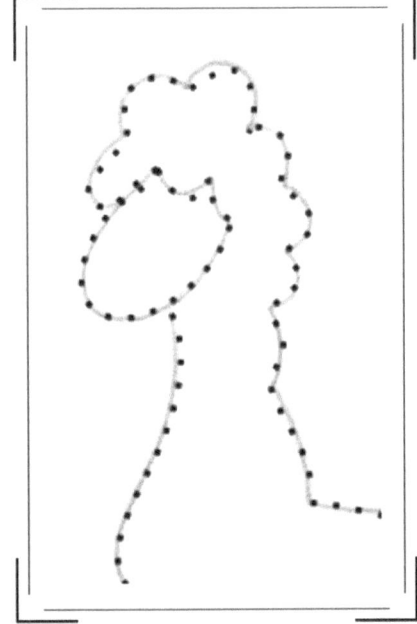

Now you try! What do your neck and head look like? Draw them below.

Next, I like to draw the body. I think of it as a large rectangle, kind of like the shape of a gift box.

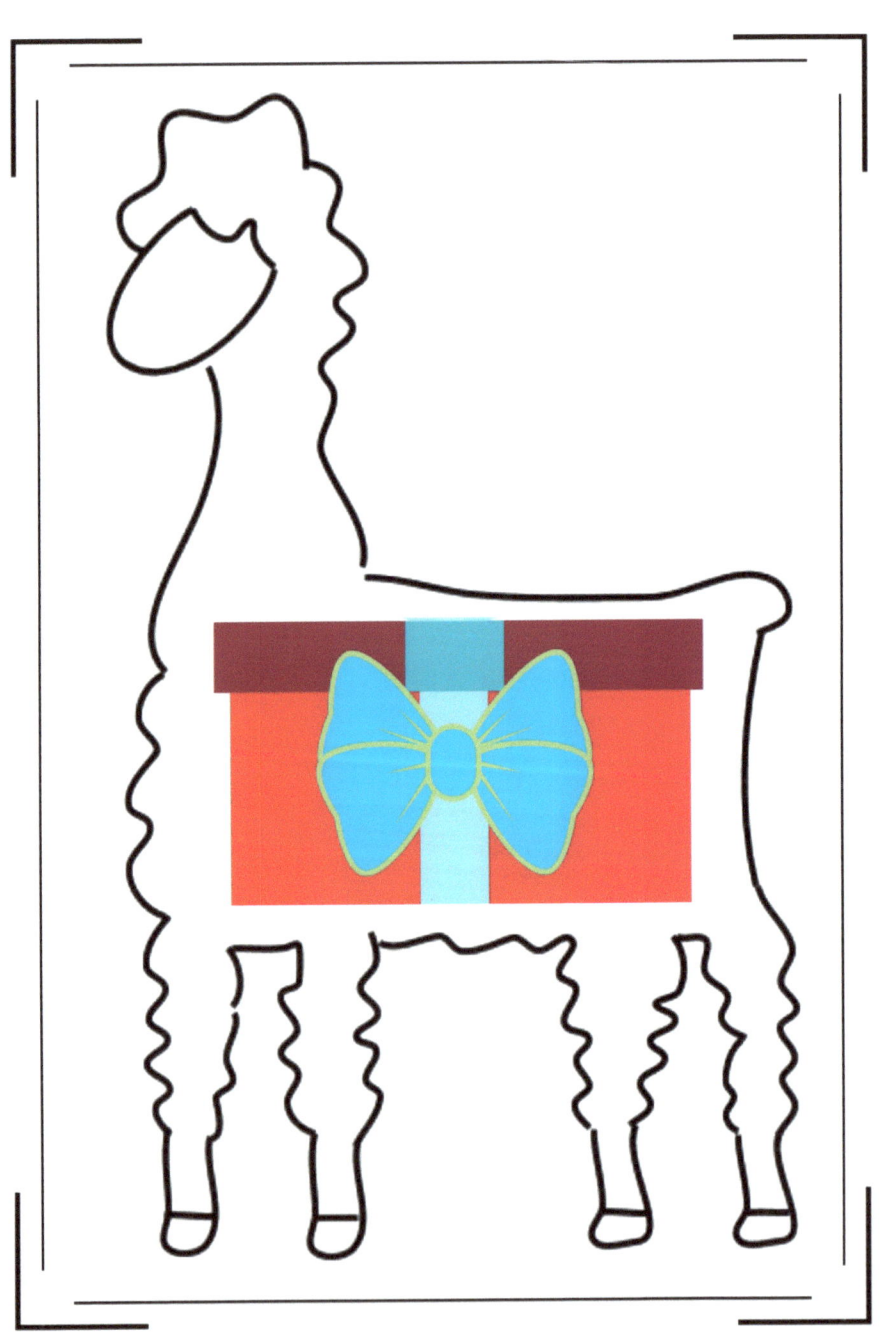

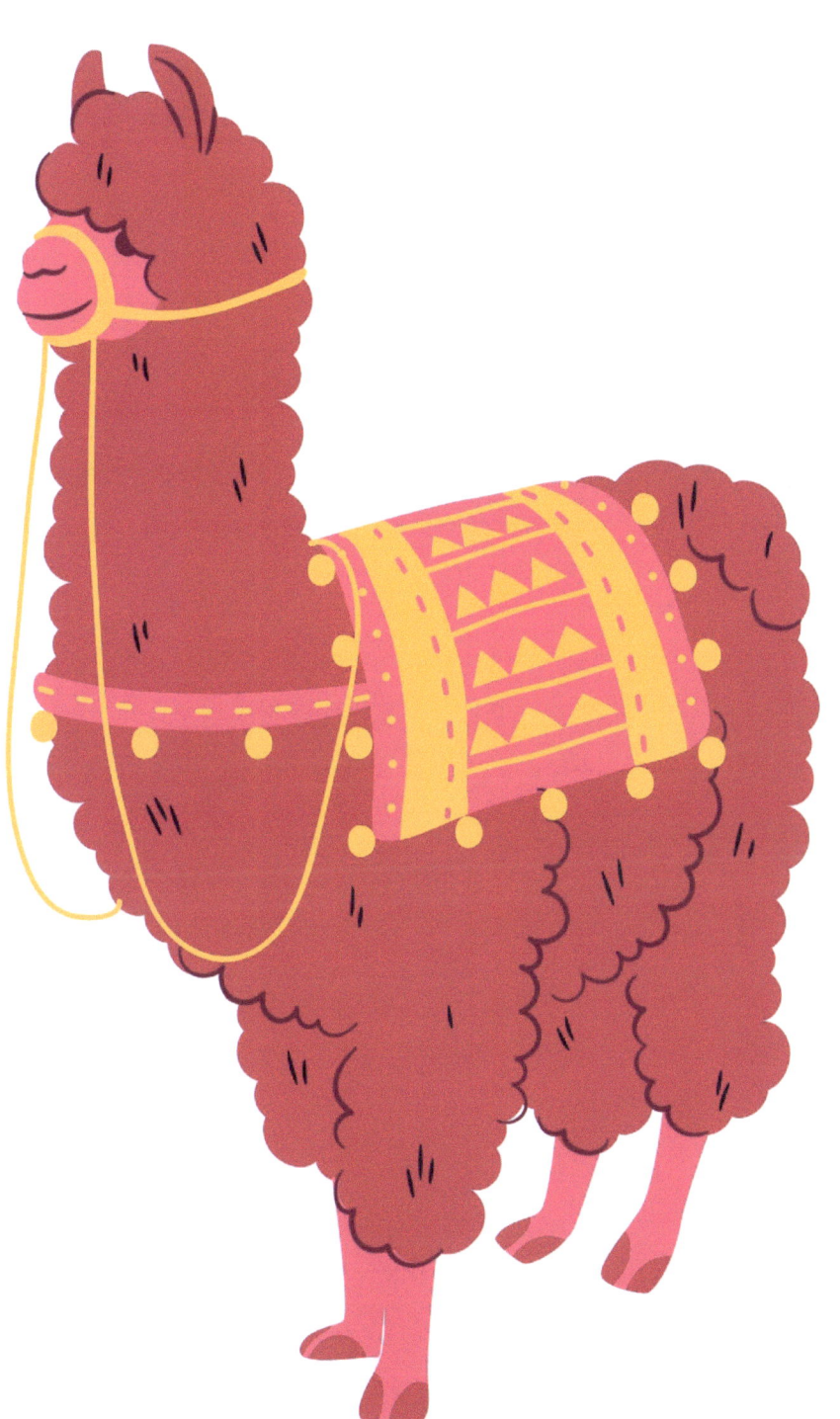

Body

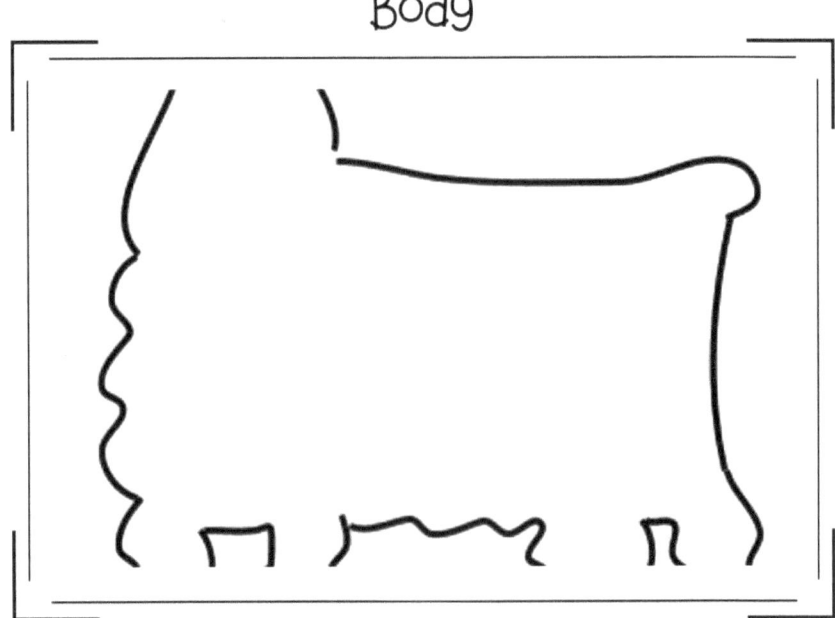

Trace it here!

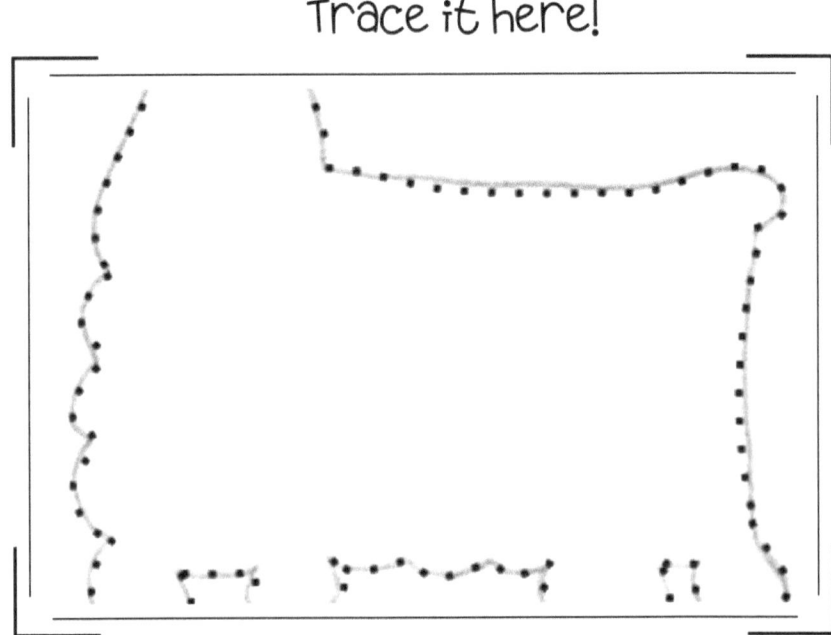

Now you try! What does your body look like? Draw it below.

Finally, I like to draw the legs and hooves. I like to imagine cotton candy on top of a thin cone.

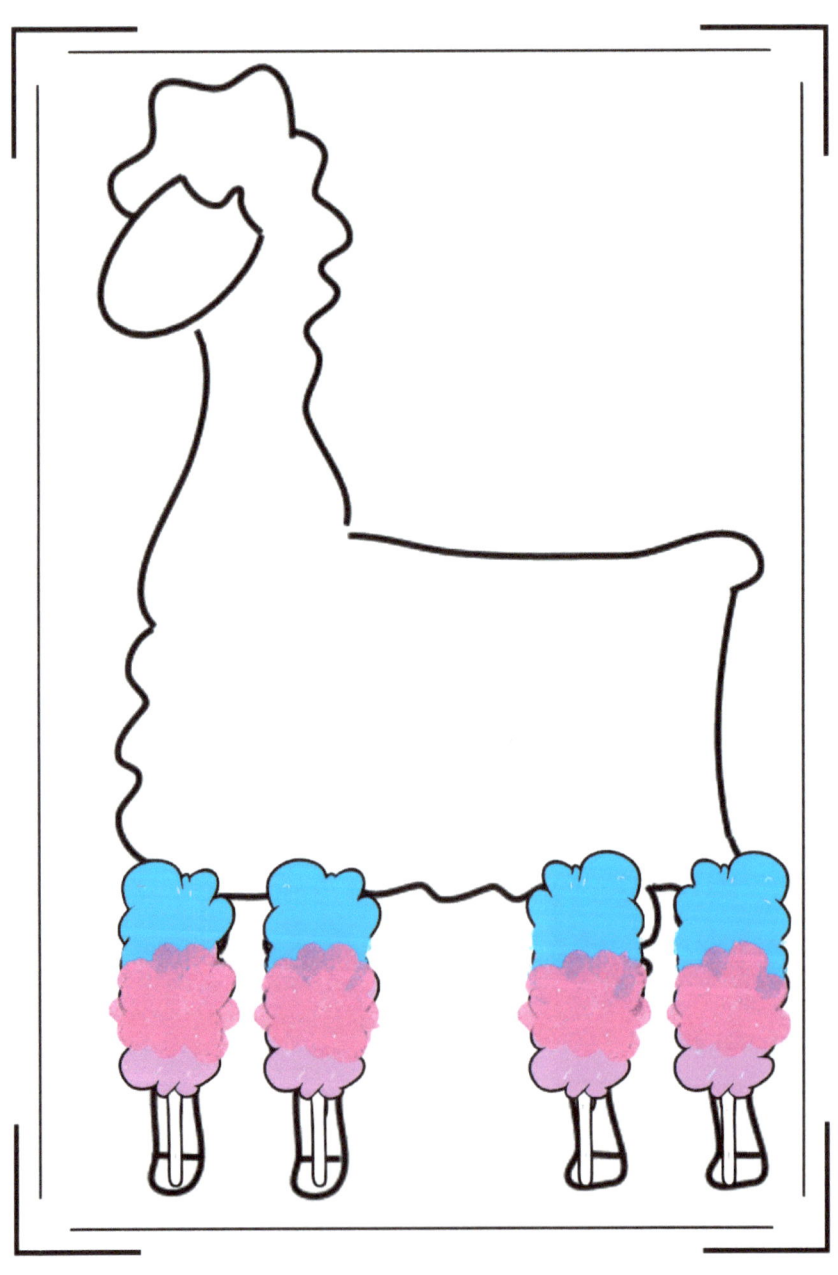

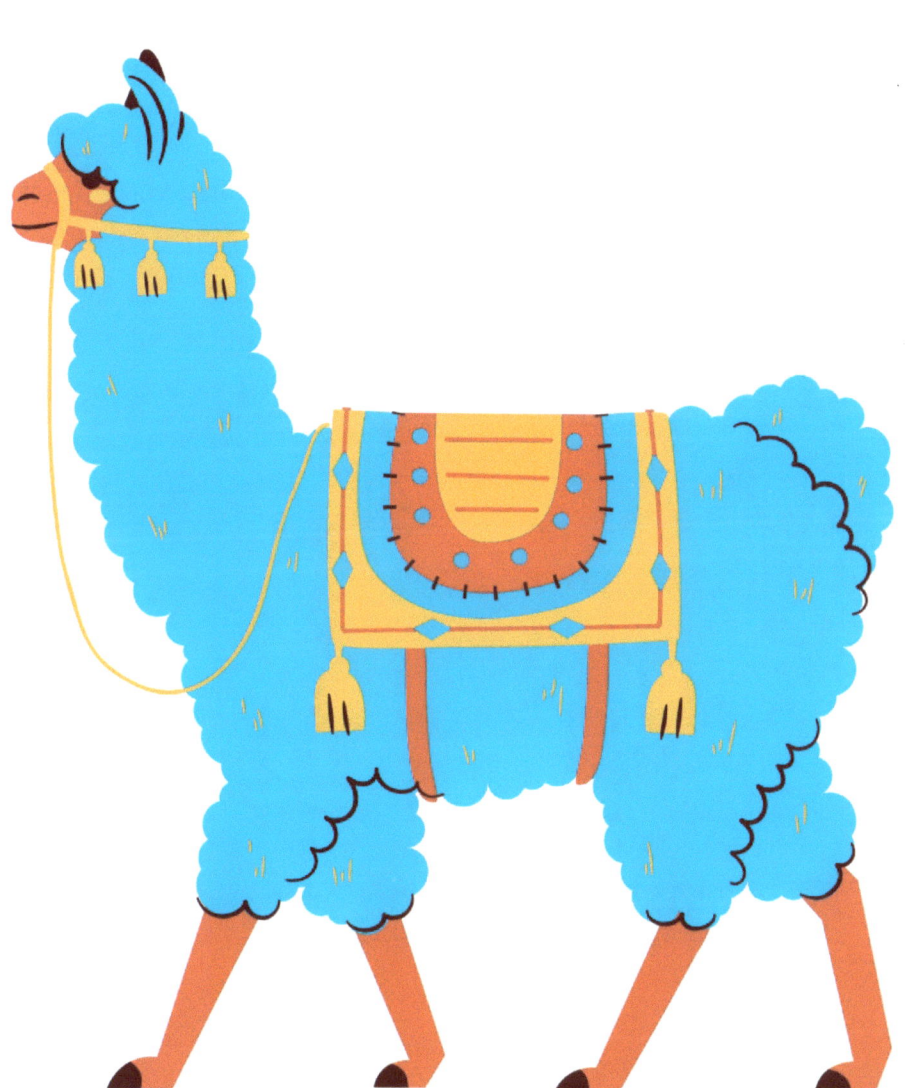

Legs/Hooves

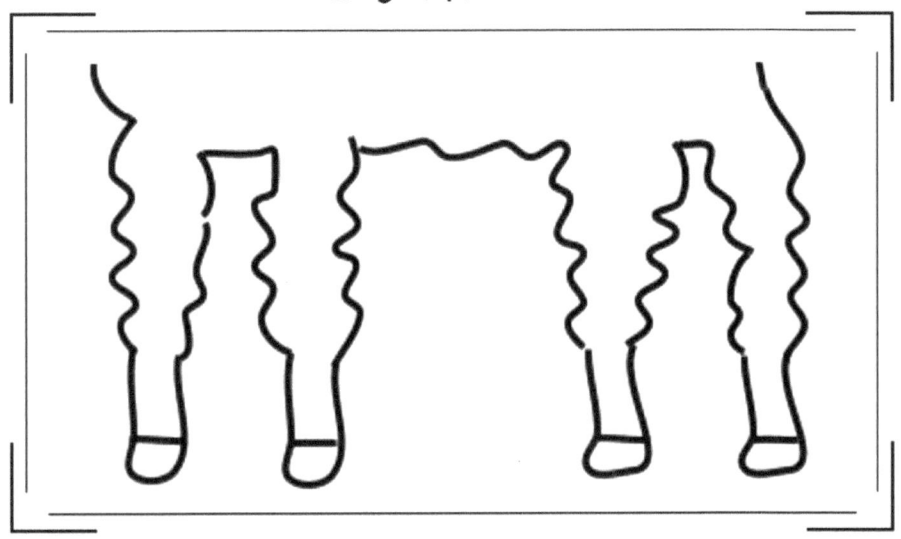

Trace it here!

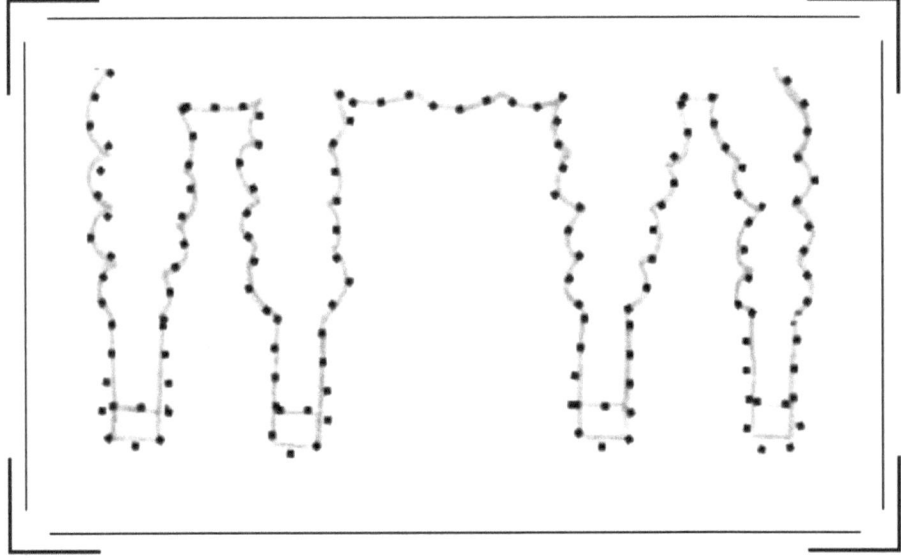

Now you try! What do your legs and hooves look like? Draw them below.

Now that we've practiced all the individual parts, it's time to put this llama together, one step at a time.

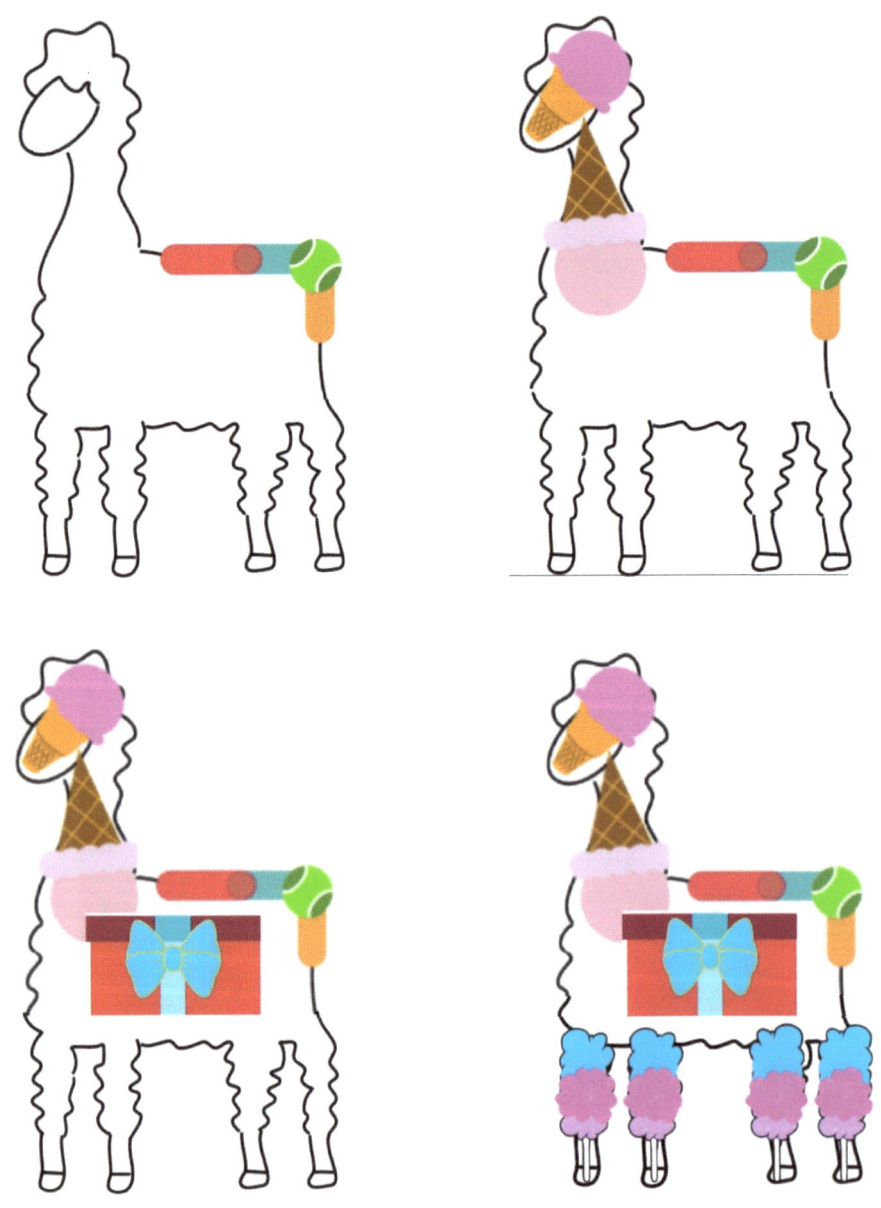

How about you give each step a try! Remember to be gentle with yourself if it doesn't come out the way you want the first time. That's why pencils have erasers! Thank goodness!

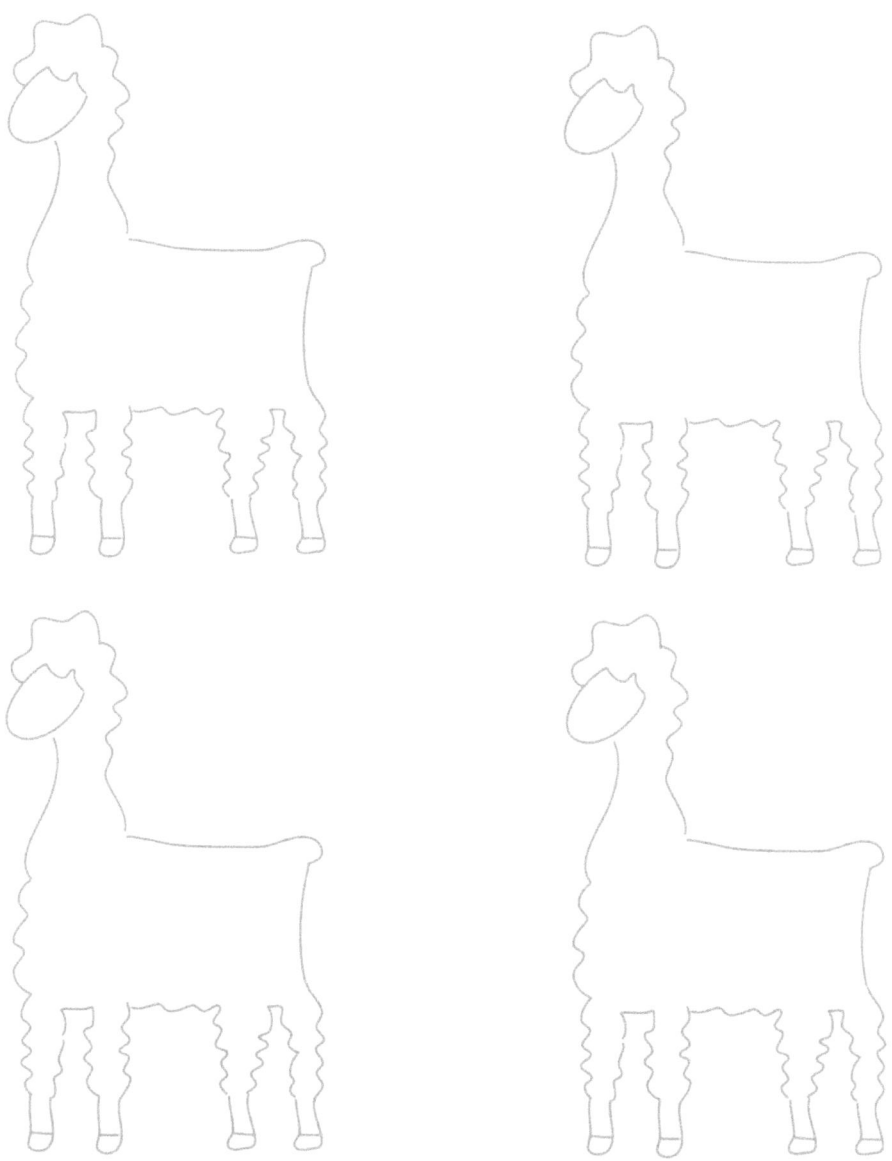

Draw-ma a Llama: Trace it here!

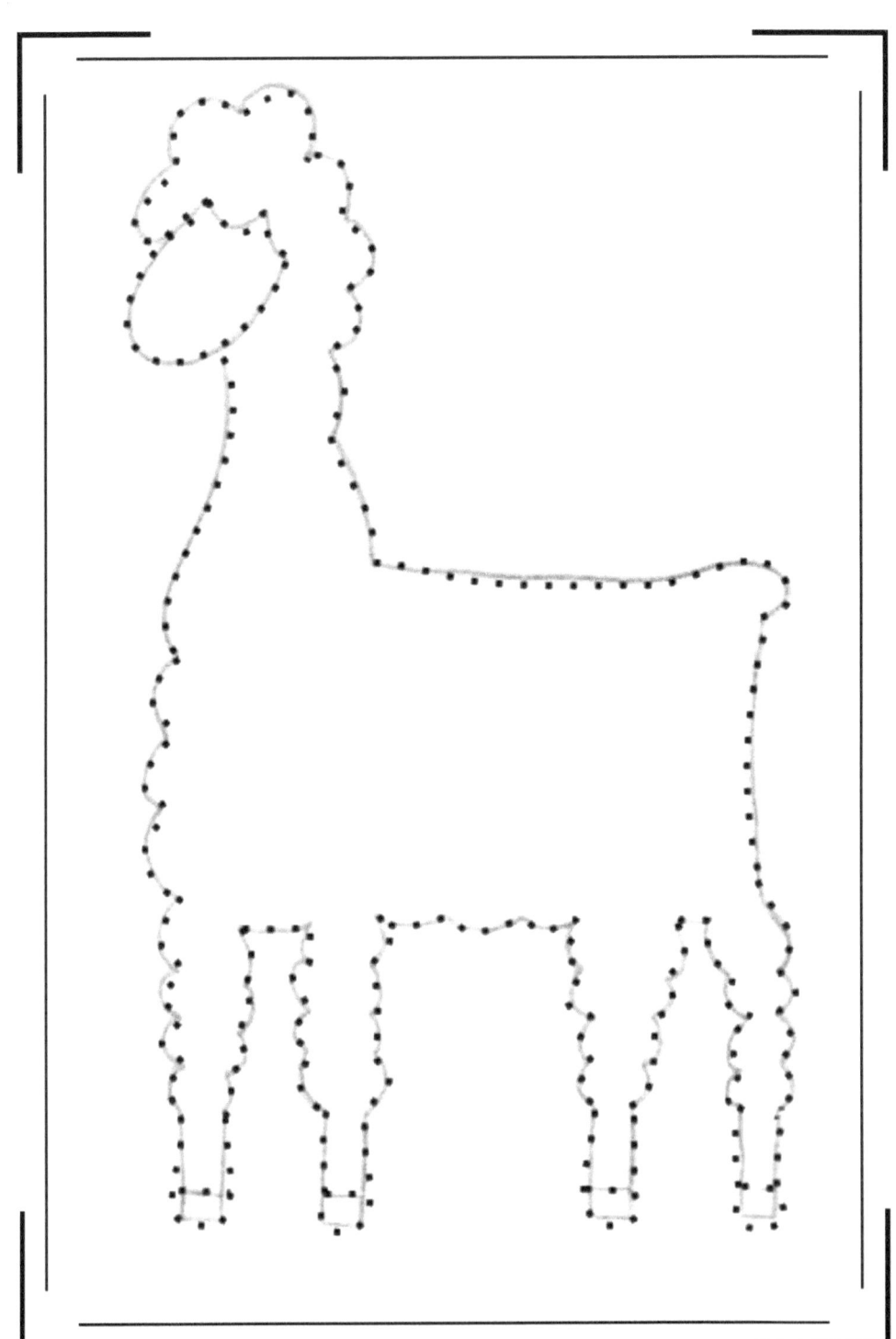

Now you try putting all the parts together into one drawing below!

You may notice your llama doesn't look quite finished. That's because we still have to make sure all our parts look well together and add details.

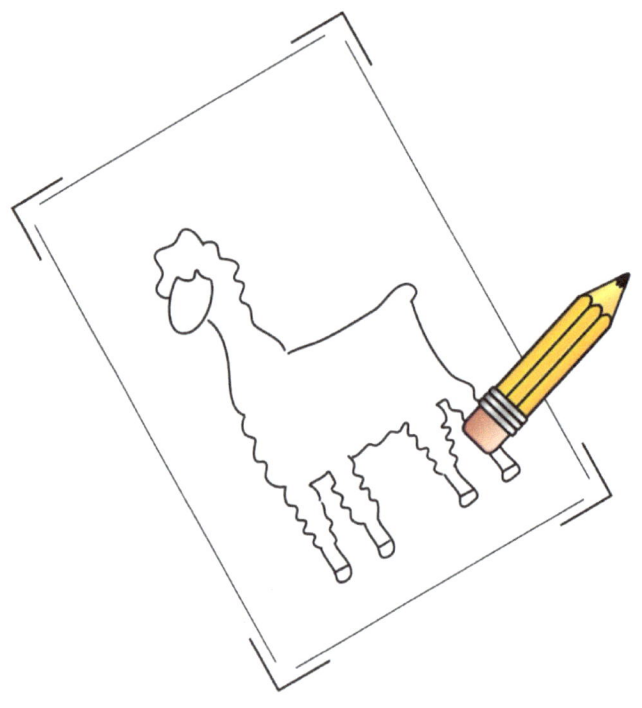

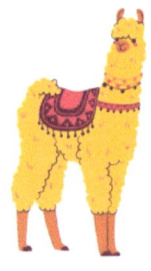

TIP: I recommend erasing any stray pencil marks now. I also like to go back and make sure there aren't any lines separating my body parts that I don't want there.

Now that you are happy with the overall look and shape of your Draw-ma Llama, it's time to go back and add some fun details! If you want your llama to look more wooly, you'll have to add little bumps that look like bunny hops. See my example below.

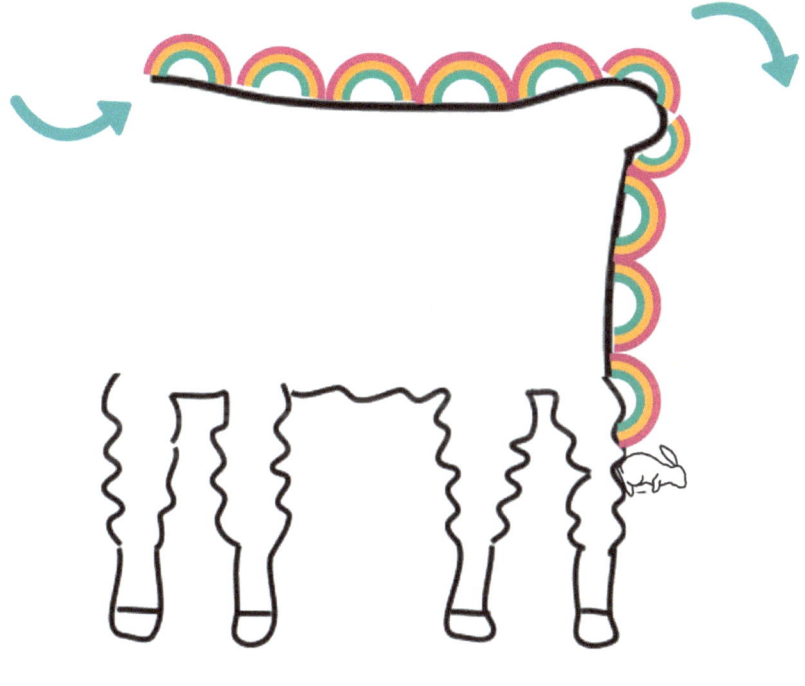

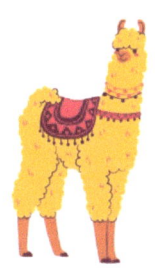

TIP: You can make your llama as wooly or smooth as you like!

You can now add details to the llama's face and add any accessories you can imagine! Does your llama have ears, or is she so wooly you can't see them? Does your llama wear jewelry, like necklaces or earrings? Does your llama have anything on his back?

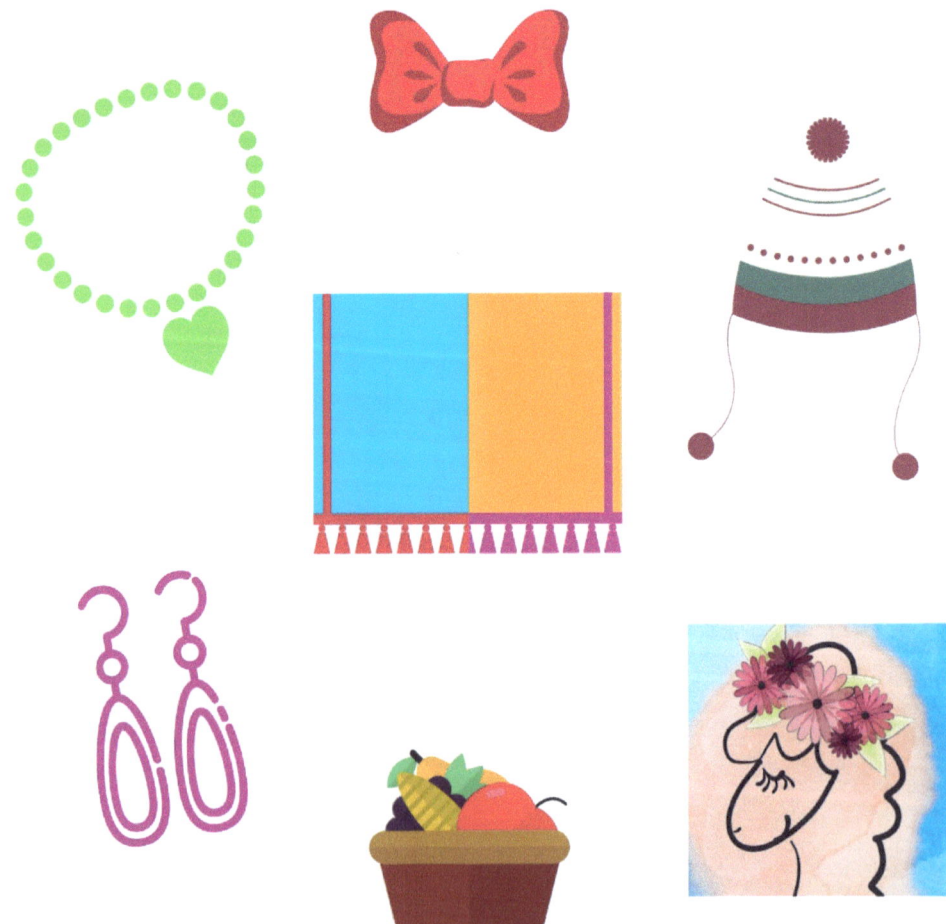

Here's my Draw-ma Llama!
Trace it here if you like!

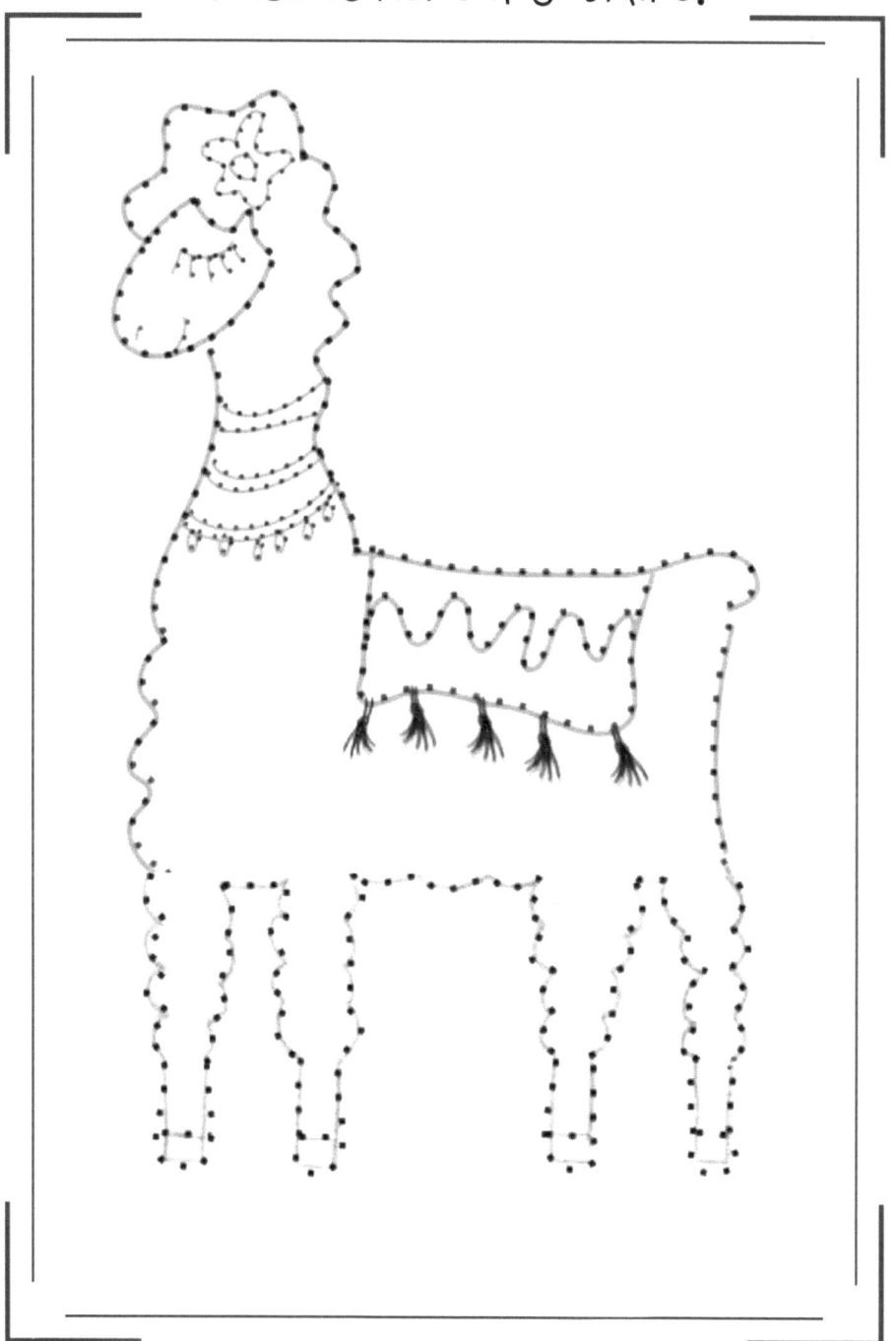

Now what does YOUR Draw-ma Llama look like? Please draw it here below! Don't forget to share it with me @authorjenniferrodriguez! I love to see your work!

Here is my original llama that I colored with my niece, Olivia, when I was still learning. It has such a special place in my heart, I used it for my book cover with some added effects!

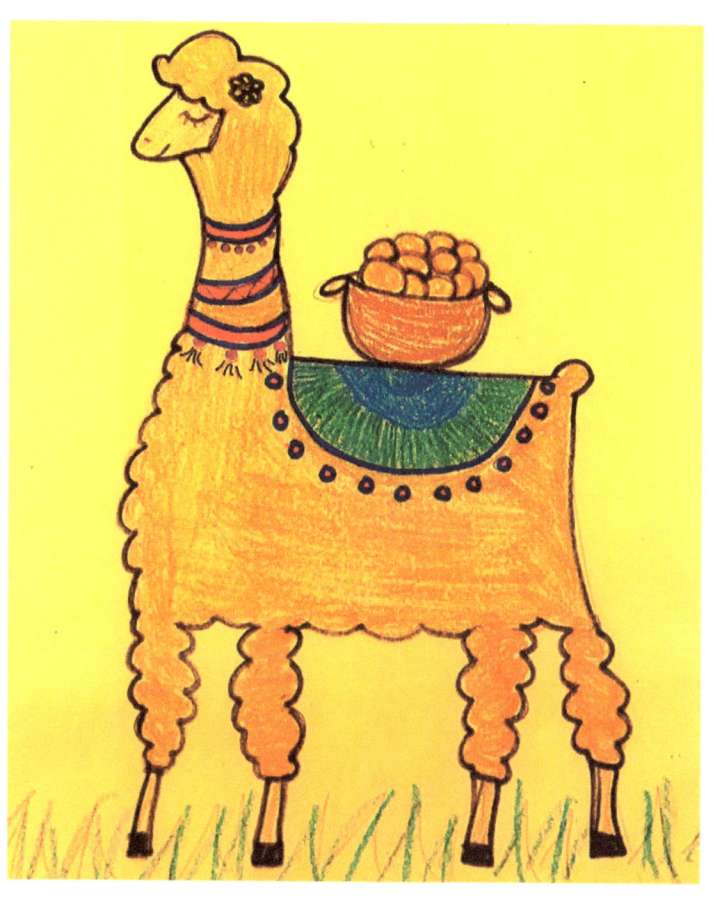

Did you Draw-ma a Llama today? Way to go! You displayed draw-some effort! Keep practicing and you'll be a Draw-ma Llama expert in no time!

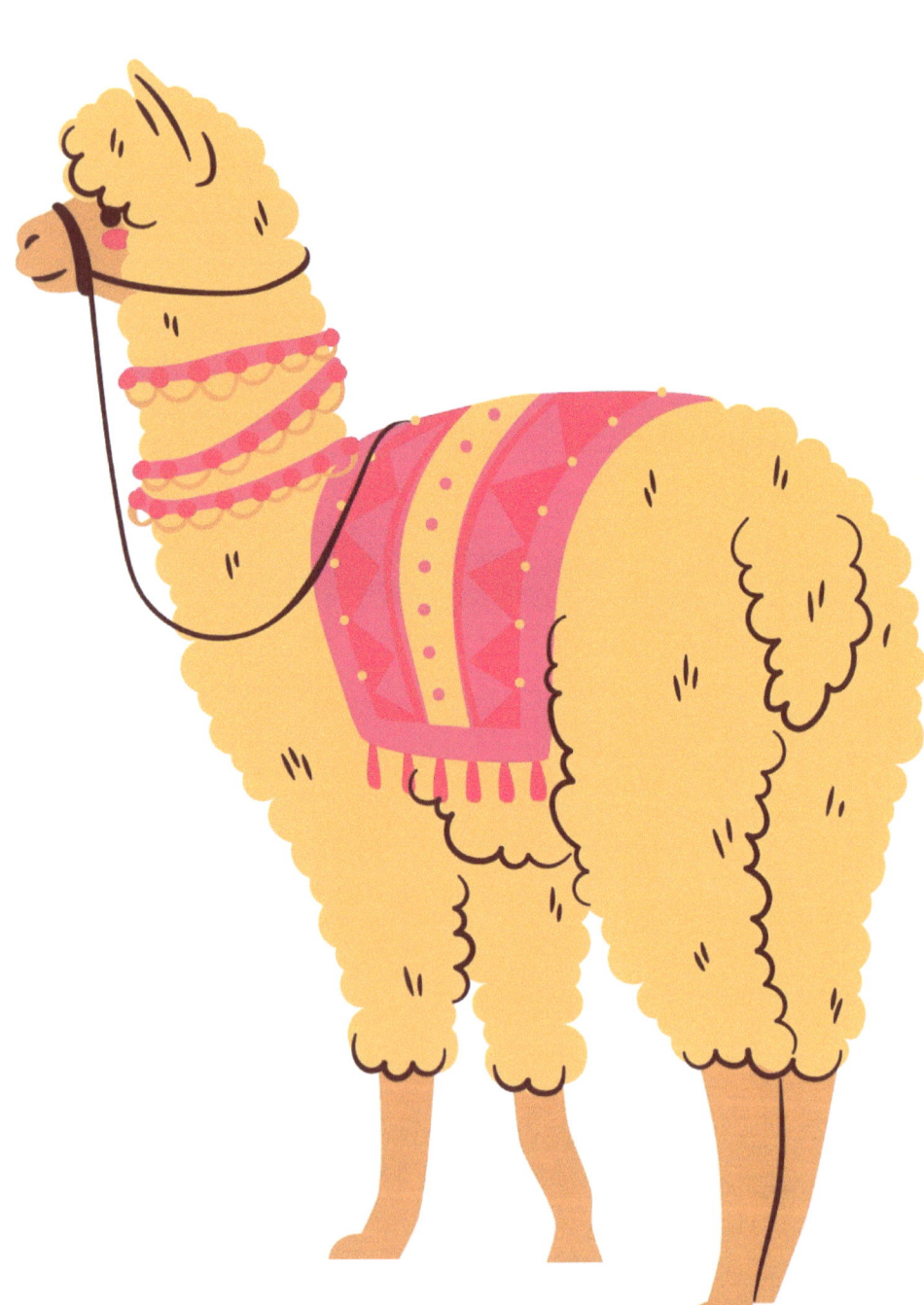

Additional coloring page

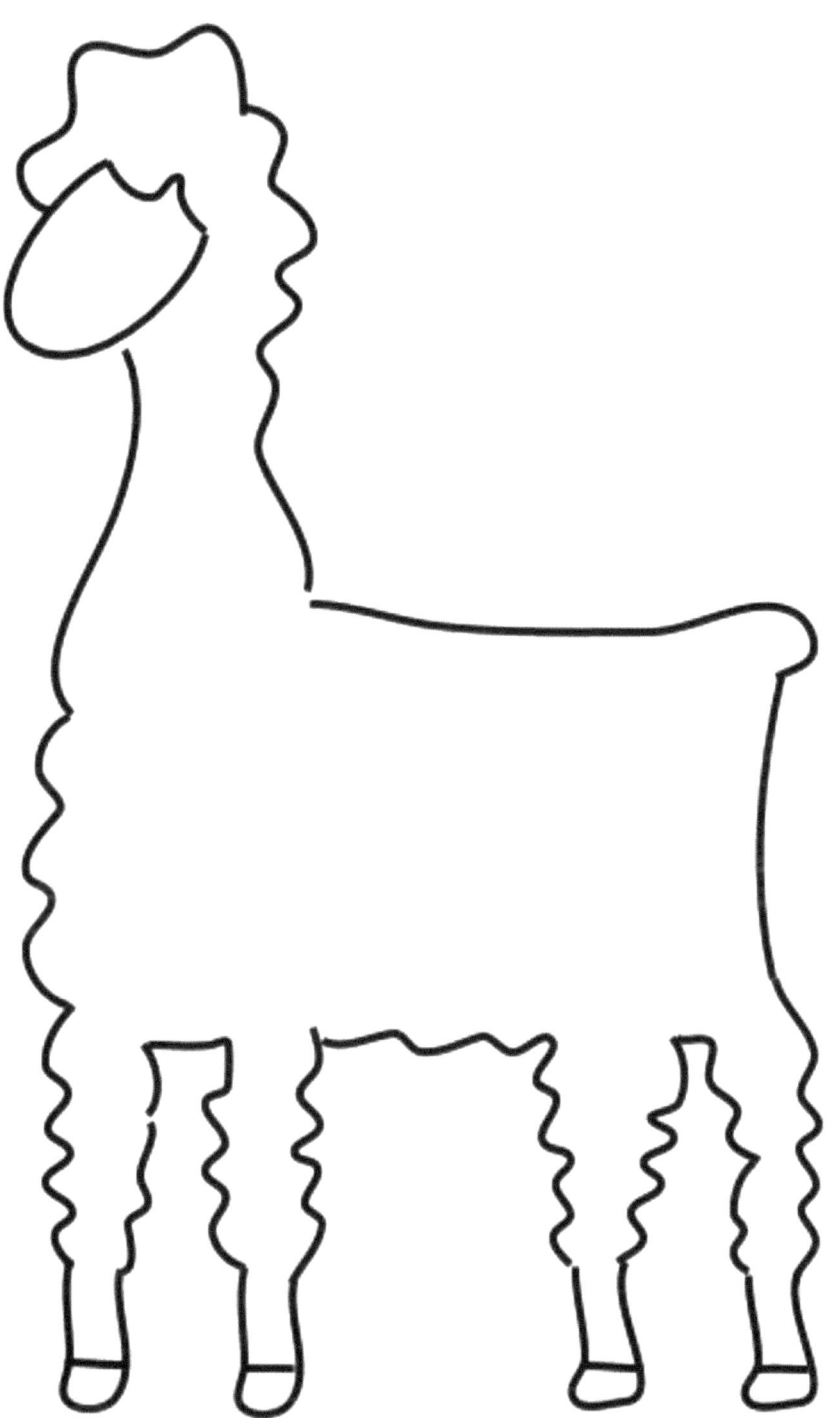

Draw-ma a Llama © Jennifer Rodriguez

Draw-ma a Llama © Jennifer Rodriguez

Additional coloring page

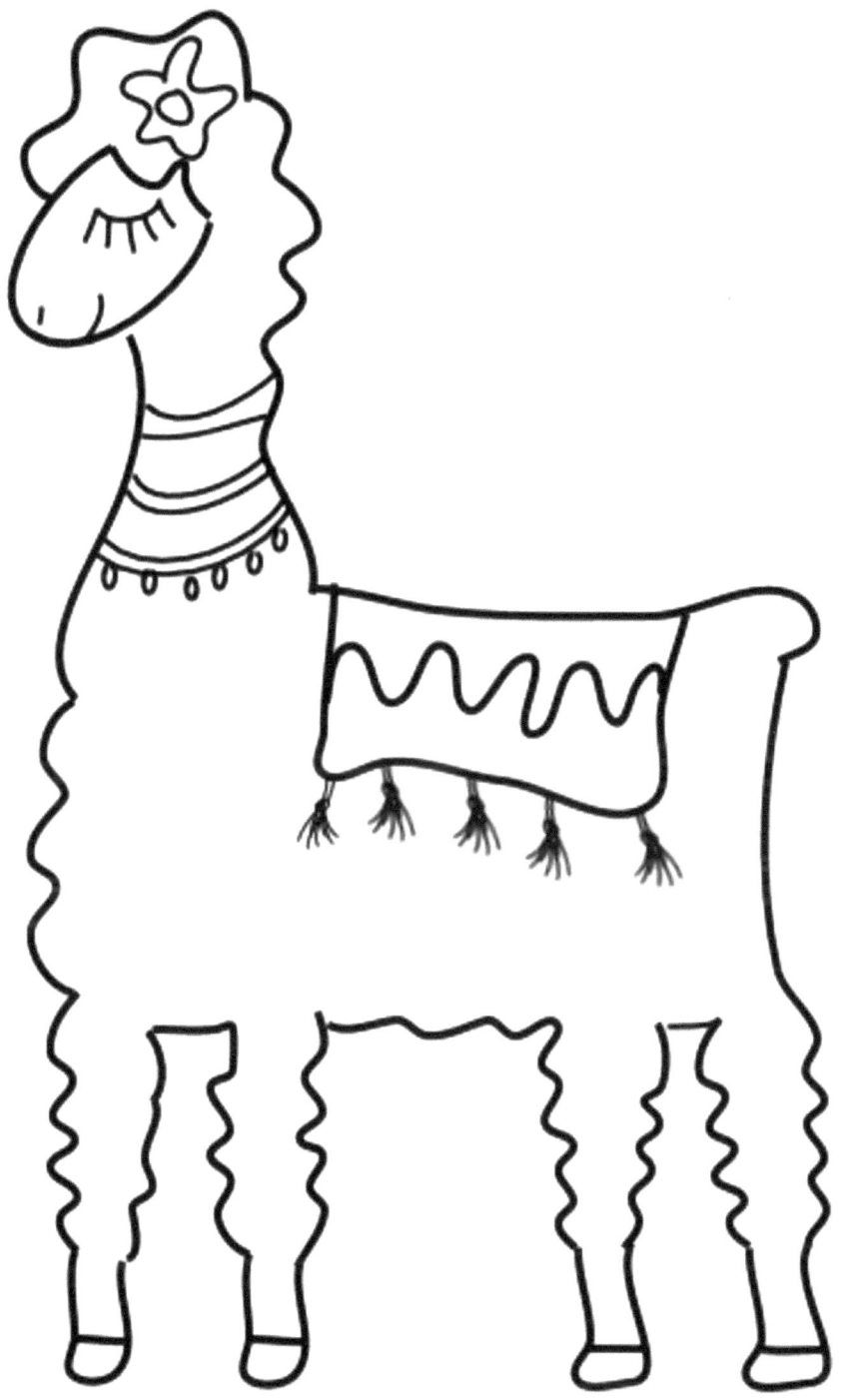

Draw-ma a Llama © Jennifer Rodriguez

Draw-ma a Llama © Jennifer Rodriguez

www.ingramcontent.com/pod-product-compliance
Lightning Source LLC
Chambersburg PA
CBHW041944240526
45473CB00033B/510